BLOOD AND FAMILY

Thomas Kinsella

Oxford   New York

OXFORD UNIVERSITY PRESS

1988

Oxford University Press, Walton Street, Oxford OX2 6DP
Oxford New York Toronto
Delhi Bombay Calcutta Madras Karachi
Petaling Jaya Singapore Hong Kong Tokyo
Nairobi Dar es Salaam Cape Town
Melbourne Auckland
and associated companies in
Berlin Ibadan

Oxford is a trade mark of Oxford University Press

This edition first published 1988 as an Oxford University Press paperback

The five sections in this book were first published in
Dublin in limited and special editions as Peppercanister
pamphlets: Peppercanister 8 'The Messenger; 9 Songs of the
Psyche; 10 Her Vertical Smile; 11 Out of Ireland;
and 12 St Catherine's Clock.

British Library Cataloguing in Publication Data
Kinsella, Thomas, 1928–
Blood and family. —— (Oxford poets).
I. Title
821'.914
ISBN 0–19–282182–2

Library of Congress Cataloging in Publication Data
Kinsella, Thomas.
Blood and family / Thomas Kinsella.
p.   cm.
I. Title
821'.914—dc19   PR6021.I35B5   1988   88–4568
ISBN 0–19–282182–2

Typeset by Wyvern Typesetting Ltd.
Printed in Great Britain by
J. W. Arrowsmith Ltd., Bristol

CONTENTS

THE MESSENGER

IN MEMORY OF
JOHN PAUL KINSELLA
DIED MAY 1976

For days I have wakened and felt immediately
half sick at something. Hour follows hour
but my shoulders are chilled with expectation.

It is more than mere Loss
                        (your tomb-image
drips and blackens, my leaden root
curled on your lap)
                   or 'what you missed'.
(The hand conceives an impossible Possible
and exhausts in mid-reach.
What could be more natural?)

Deeper. A suspicion in the bones
as though they too could melt in filth.

Something to discourage goodness.

A moist movement within.
A worm winds on its hoard.
A rim of hide lifts like a lip.

A dead egg glimmers — a pearl in muck
glimpsed only as the muck settles.
The belly settles and crawls tighter.

I

His mother's image settled on him
out of the dark, at the last,
and the Self sagged, unmanned.

Corded into a thick dressing gown
he glared from his rocker
at people *whispering* on television.

He knocked the last drops of Baby Power
into his glass and carried the lifewater
to his lips. He recollected himself

and went on with a story out of Guinness's
— the Brewery pension 'abated' by 'an amount
equal to the amount' of some pittance

on some Godforsaken pretext.
His last battle — the impulse
at its tottering extreme:

muster your fellow pensioners, and advance
pitched with them
                    ('Power to the Spent!')

against the far off boardroom door.
All about him, open mouthed,
they expired in ones and twos.

Somebody well dressed
pressed my hand in the graveyard.
A thoughtful delegated word or two:

'His father before him ... Ah, the barge captain ...
A valued connection. He will be well remembered ...
He lived in his two sons.'

In his own half fierce force
he lived! And stuck
the first brand shakily

4

under that good family firm,
formed their first Union,
and entered their lists.

Mason and Knight
gave ground in twostep,
manager and priest disappeared

and reappeared under each other's hats;
the lumpenproletariat
stirred truculently and settled;

in jigtime, to the ever popular
Faith Of Our Fathers, he was high and dry.
And in time was well remembered.

In front of the fireplace, florid and with scorn,
in his frieze jacket, with a couple of bottles
of Export in the pockets, he stomached it.

Thumbs in belt, back and forth
in stiff boots he rocked with the news
(I care) (But accept) (I reject)

in full vigour, in his fiftieth year,
every ounce of youth
absorbed into his body.

For there is really nothing to be done.
There is an urge, and it is valuable,
but it is of no avail.

He brandished his solid body
thirty feet high above their heads therefore
and with a shout of laughter

traversed a steel beam in the Racking Shed
and dared with outstretched arms
what might befall.

And it befell, that summer,
after the experimental doses,
that his bronchi wrecked him with coughs

and the muffled inner
heartstopping little
hammerblows began.

*

A brave leap   On bright prospects
in full heart   sable: a slammed
into full stop.   door.

Vaunt and check.
Cursus inter-
ruptus.

Typically, there is a turning away.
The Self is islanded in fog.
It is meagre and plagued with wants

but secure. Every positive matter
that might endanger — but also enrich —
is banished. The banished matter

(a cyst, in effect, of the subject's aspirations
painful with his many disappointments)
absorbs into the psyche, where it sleeps.

Intermittently, when disturbed, it wakes
as a guardian — or 'patron' — monster
with characteristic conflicting emotional claims:

appalling, appealing; exacting sympathy
even as it threatens. (Our verb 'to haunt'
preserves the ambiguity exactly.)

Somewhere on the island, Cannibal
lifts his halved head and bellows
with incompleteness . . . Or better —

a dragon slashes its lizard wings uneasily
as it looks out and smells the fog
and itches and hungers in filth and fire.

*

Often, much too familiar for comfort,
the beast was suddenly there
insinuating between us:

'Who'd like to know what *I* know?'
'Who has a skeleton in *his* meat cupboard?'

'Who is inclined to lapse and let
the bone go with the dog?'

'Who flings off in a huff
and never counts the cost
as long as there's a bitter phrase
to roll around on the tongue?'

'When Guess Who polished his pointy shoe
and brushed his brilliantine
to whose admiring gaze
guess who hoodwinked Who?'

Or it would sigh and say:
'Guess who'd love to gobble *you* up . . . !'
Or 'Who'd like to see what *I* have?'

*

I would. And have followed
the pewtery heave of hindquarters
into the fog, the wings down at heel,

until back there in the dark
the whole thing
fell on its face.

And blackened. . . And began
melting its details and dripping them away
little by little to reveal

him (supine, jutjawed and
incommunicable, privately
surrendering his tissues and traps).

And have watched my hand reach in under
after something, and felt it
close upon it and ease him of it.

The eggseed Goodness
that is also called
Decency.

II

Goodness is where you find it.
Abnormal.
       A pearl.

A milkblue
blind orb.
       Look in it:

It is outside the Black Lion, in Inchicore.
A young man. He is not much more than thirty.
He is on an election lorry, trying to shout.

He is goodlooking and dark.
He has a raincoat belted tight
and his hair is brushed back, like what actor . . .

He is shouting about the Blueshirts
but his voice is hoarse.
His arm keeps pointing upward.

I am there. A dark little
blackvelvet-eyed jew-child
with leaflets.

A big Dublin face
leans down with a moustache, growling
it is a scandal.

                *

The Oblate Fathers was packed.
I sat squeezed against a cold pillar.
A bull-voice rang among the arches.

An old turkey-neck in front, with a cured boil
on top of the collar, kept swallowing.
A woman whispered in my back hair.

I made faces at my ghost in the brawn marble.
The round shaft went up shining
into a mouth of stone flowers

9

and the angry words echoed among
the hanging lamps, off the dark golden walls,
telling every Catholic how to vote.

He covered my hand with his
and we started getting out
in the middle of Mass past everybody.

Father Collier's top half in the pulpit
in a muscular black soutane and white lace
grabbed the crimson velvet ledge

— thick white hair, glasses,
a red face, a black mouth —
shouting Godless Russia at us.

It is an August evening, in Wicklow.
It is getting late. They have tussled in love.
They are hidden, near the river bank.

They lie face up in the grass, not touching,
head close to head, a woman and her secret husband.
A gossamer ghost arrows and hesitates

out of the reeds, and stands in the air above them
insect-shimmering, and settles on a bright
inner upturn of her dress. The wings

close up like palms. The body, a glass worm,
is pulsing. The tail-tip winces and quivers:

I *think* this is where I come in . . .

Trailing a sunless instinct,
a saw-jawed multiple past,
an edible (almost liquid)
vulnerability,
and winged! — weightless and wondrous! —
up from the bloodied slime
through the arms of a black rainbow
scooping down in beauty
he has come, he has arisen
out of the pool of night!

It is! It is!
        Hurry!
says the great womb-whisper.
Quick!
        I am all egg!

Inside, it is bare but dimly alive.
Such light as there is comes in overcast
through a grey lace curtain across the window,

diffuses in the dust above the bench
and shows him stooped over his last
in a cobbler's shop. He is almost still a boy:

his hands are awkwardly readying something,
his face and shoulders are soft-handsome,
pale silver, ill at ease

in the odour-bearing light. The rest is obscure,
swallowed back in man-smells
of leather and oily metal, and the faintest

musk. Beside him, his father's leaden skull
is inclined, gentle and deaf,
above the work on his apron.

The old lion-shoulders expand in the Guinness jersey,
the jaws work in his cheeks
as the quivering awl

pierces the last hole in a sole with a grunt.
He wheezes and pulls it out, and straightens.
The tide is rising and the river runs fast

into the middle span of the last bridge.
He touches the funnel on a nerve at the base
and doffs it on its hinge at the last instant

— the smoke occluding — and hauls it up again
gleaming and pluming in open water.
Here and there along the Liffey wall

he is acclaimed in friendly mockery,
humbly, saturninely, returned. . .
He reaches for needle and thread

patiently, as his son
struggles at the blank iron foot
in his father's den.

He will not stick at this . . . The knife-blades,
the hammers and pincers, the rasps and punches,
the sprigs in their wooden pits,

catching the light on the plank bench
among uppers and tongues and leather scraps
and black stumps of heelball.

He reaches for a hammer,
his jaw jutting as best it can
with Marx, Engels, Larkin

howling with upstretched arms into the teeth
of Martin Murphy and the Church
and a flourish of police batons,

Connolly strapped in a chair
regarding the guns
that shall pronounce his name for ever.

Baton struck,
                    gun spat,
and Martin Murphy shall change his hat.

Son and father, upright, right arms raised.
Stretching a thread.
Trying to strike right.

Deeper. The room where they all lived
behind the shop. It is dark here too — shut off
by the narrow yard. But it doesn't matter:

it is bustling with pleasure.
A new messenger boy
stands there in uniform, with shining belt!

He is all excitement: arms akimbo,
a thumb crooked by the telegram pouch,
shoes polished, and a way to make in the world.

His eyes are bright,
his schoolmaster's tags fresh in mind.
He has a few of the Gentlemen's Sixpenny Library

under the bed — *A Midsummer Night's Dream*,
Sartor Resartus, *The Divine Comedy*, with a notebook,
Moore's *Melodies*, a trifle shaken . . . Shelley, unbound . . .

He unprops the great Post Office bicycle
from the sewing machine and wheels it through the passage
by odours of apron and cabbage-water and whitewashed damp

through the shop and into the street.
It faces uphill. The urchin mounts. I see
a flash of pedals! And a clean pair of heels!

A cross grain of impotent anger. About it
the iridescent, untouchable secretions
collect. It is a miracle:

membrane and mineral in precious combination.
An eye, pale with strain, forms in the dark.
The oddity nestles in slime

functionless, in all its rarity,
purifying nothing. But nothing can befoul it
— which ought probably to console.

He rolled on rubber tyres
out of the chapel door. The oak box
paused gleaming in the May morning air

and turned, sensing its direction.
Our scattered tribe began gathering itself
and trudged off onto a gravel path after it.

By their own lightness
four girls and three boys separated themselves
in a ragged band out from our dull custom

and moved up close after it, in front,
all shapes and sizes,
grandchildren, colourful and silent.

SONGS OF THE PSYCHE

SETTINGS

Model School, Inchicore

Miss Carney handed us out blank paper and marla,
old plasticine with the colours
all rolled together into brown.

You started with a ball of it
and rolled it into a snake curling
around your hand, and kept rolling it
in one place until it wore down into two
with a stain on the paper.

We always tittered at each other
when we said the adding-up table in Irish
and came to her name.

*

In the second school we had Mr Browne.
He had white teeth in his brown man's face.

He stood in front of the black board
and chalked a white dot.

    'We are going to start
       decimals.'

    I am going to know
       everything.

*

One day he said:
'Out into the sun!'
We settled his chair under a tree
and sat ourselves down delighted
in two rows in the greeny gold shade.

A fat bee floated around
shining amongst us
and the flickering sun
warmed our folded coats
and he said: 'History . . . !'

*

When the Autumn came
and the big chestnut leaves
fell all over the playground
we piled them in heaps
between the wall and the tree trunks
and the boys ran races
jumping over the heaps
and tumbled into them shouting.

*

I sat by myself in the shed
and watched the draught
blowing the papers
around the wheels of the bicycles.

Will God judge
    our most secret thoughts and actions?
God will judge
    our most secret thoughts and actions
and every idle word that man shall speak
he shall render an account of it
on the Day of Judgment.

*

The taste
of ink off
the nib shrank your
mouth.

Phoenix Street

It was dark everywhere.
The two paths were empty.
All in.
All in.

*

I have climbed the narrow turn
of the top stairs, holding
the banisters draped with
trousers and pullovers,
and stood smelling the landing again.

And I have opened the black-stained
double doors of the triangular
press up in the corner,
and his dark nest
stirred with promises:

Ruskin and Engels and Carlyle;
Shakespeare in tiny print,
1927 in dead pencil;

the insurance collection book
in a fat elastic band;
a brown photograph

with four young men
dressed up together
and leaning together in laughter.

Bow Lane

I poked in at the back corner
of the wardrobe, at the blind
standing rolled up. It rustled
like a bat trapped inside.

There was light still coming in
over Corcorans' wall
up to the Blessed Virgin on the shelf
over the grandparents' bed.

They kept Uncle Tom's painting
hanging in there, in a black frame
— a steamer with three funnels,
and TK painted on the foam.

He died in here in 1916
of cancer of the colon. My father heard him
whispering to himself: 'Jesus,
Jesus, let me off.' But nothing worked.

I took the grey animal book
from under the clothes in the drawer
and opened it at the Capuchin monkeys
in their forest home.

I asked Tom Ryan once: 'Tell me the print!'
but he only grinned and said
'I will if you can spell Wednesday.'
With his slithery walk . . .

They were lighting the lamps
outside in the shop and she started shouting:
'What are you up to in there?
Always stuck in that old room.'

INVOCATION

Sweet mother, sweet muscle,
predatrix,

always in the midst
yet walking to one side

silent, reticent, rarely seen
yet persistent,

we implore — the subsequent
bustling in the previous:

Judge not.
But judge.

SONGS OF THE PSYCHE

I

A character, indistinct, entered,
looked about him, and began:

Why had I to wait until I am graceless,
unsightly, and a little nervous of stooping
until I could see

through these clear eyes I had once?
It is time. And I am
shivering as in stupid youth.

Who have stood where I was born
and snapped my bitten fingers!

II

It was time.
           To settle in
and feel what it is like
to be half safe.

When I think of what I *could* . . .
My brain hammers, and I could
dance!
          But I settled back and
turned inward.

I smelled at a crack in the dirt
and was taken away
teeth grinding
and eyes alight.

An unholy muttering
lingered on my palms
as I laid them to my cheeks
and slept.

III

(Chew nine times
on the chosen meat
and set it down
outside her door

then when you wake
rat small, rat still,
you will carry her life
in your palms, rat self.)

IV

There are certain
ill-chosen spirits

that cower close
on innermost knowledge

and must burrow with special care
to find the shallowest peace.

Their need binds them
and hangs between them.

In special tenderness and mental fire
these wound each other

with every touch
meditative and brutal:

they have eaten
and must eat.

V

What a thing it is
to know a thing
full fifty years

with kindness as of one thing
for another
of only its kind.

A monster bore me
and I bear
a monster with me.

VI

I have kissed the inner earth
and the grin of stone upon stone
and it was time again

to surrender
to your
beaten smile

VII

And she came by a little-haunted path
with modest run advancing
dancing in her flowers
awkwardly up to me.

                    It was something
to take a little of the spring
out of a person's step . . .
She offered me her hands.

I took them in mine
— averse
          but it was enough:
we were no longer two

but a third
          fumbling
ghost at polite ghost
of its own matter.

VIII

A tree with a twisted trunk;
two trees grown into one.
A heart-carving grown thick,
the cuts so deep.

The leaves reached out past us
and hissed: *We were so fond of you!*
There was a stir of flower heads
about our feet

gold for the first blaze,
red for the rough response,
dark blue for misunderstanding,
jet black for rue,   ￼

pale for the
unfinished children
that are
waiting everywhere

IX

Night foxes
body masks

tilted up, eyes
a city of lights

a cistern hiss
in their erect ears

they are dreaming
one another

X

The fire was banked,
the kitchen door half open,
the chairs angled where they were left.

A moth fumbled with its
fragile blur up
the tobacco-smelling chimney-corner.

Tireless and lifespans old
the long clock-stick laboured
over the mantelpiece, forth and back.

Behind the kitchen table
with the apron
folded on the butter bowl

they returned into the dark
with murder and girl robbery
in their hearts.

*

A great delicate self
approached her cold face

toward the window,
cheek wide and glowing,

afloat, bright, an O
stopped,

a whole mind
blind overhead.

Pegged to a rafter, bathed in smoke,
splayed in flight,

a great moth of prey,
flat, with excavated breast,

come from nowhere,
stared back.

*

A silk maggot,
a detached hair

bathed in firelight,
I writhed with memory.

XI

Come with me
　o'er the crystal stream
where eyelids dart
　in the dappled shallows

to where you wait
　on the farther bank
troubled and pretty
　with tattered basket.

Your feathery flesh
　I will kneel and kiss.
Your slender bones
　I will take in mine.

I will pick a straw
　from your stiffened dress
and so retire
　while the grasses whisper

and leeches wrinkle
　black in the water,
willow leaves
　that have fed on blood.

XII

It is time, the night
gone, first light
fidgetting under the leaves.

Let us kneel
and rinse the crust from the cup.

XIII

I woke suffocating,
  slipped through a fault
into total dark.

No.

I came to myself
  in the middle of a dark wood,
electric with hope.

Please . . .

Yet it *is*
  a matter of
negative release:

of being thrown
  up out of a state of storm
into a state of peace

or sleep,
  or a dream,
or a system of dreams.

By normal process
  organic darkness,
in potentia all things,

would summon
  Self firstly into being,
a Shadow *in actu*,

an upright on a flat plain,
  a bone stirs
in first clay

and a beam of light struck
  and snaked glittering across a surface
in multi-meanings and vanishes.

Then stealers of fire;
     dragon slayers; helpful animals;
and ultimately the Cross.

Unless the thing were to be based
     on sexuality
or power.

NOTES

A New Beginning

God is good but
He had to start
somewhere out of the ache
of *I am*

and lean Himself
over the mothering pit
in faith
thinking

a mouth
to My kiss
in opening

let there be
remote

Opposites

Love is refreshment
in the recognition of pattern.

Grudging memory is its opposite:
it is revealed in the lips.

Our mouths locked in privacy.
The shadow pattern shifted.

The Little Children

I held her propped
        by the tip of a blunt love finger
against the kitchen wall
        and let her topple forward

one, two, three!
        in laughter and panic
into darkness and fire.

*

Incurious about his own
        breaking and renewing
energies, his developing
        and abandoned purposes,

he fixes the pieces
        in and upon each other
in a series of beginnings

with feathery touches
        and brutal fumblings,
in stupefying waste,
        brooding and light.

*

At the first trace
        of backward pressure
the child grows unusable.

Brotherhood

I stretched out
my hand to you. Brother.

The reason for the impulse
was unclear:

your behaviour and your work
are incomprehensible to me.

But I had offered my hand.
We were joined by the soft leather of palms.

The matter resolved itself.
A voice whispered:

It is Spring
and no time for kindness;

we must bear in mind
the quality of the Fall.

I dropped your hand.

Talent and Friendship

Neither is simple
and neither is handed down.

Either persisted in without change
grows ridiculous

and either at any time
may fail.

If it fail in part
it is made good only in part

and if it come to final failure
accept — but prepare for a difficult widow:

that fig-bodied stone devil
on your sanctuary wall

gross mouth open
to all comers

or, as I remember,
a still youthful witch

moving off sick to death
among the graves and the old men

in sharp argument with her pale son,
he muttering in sharp answer,

deadly familiar,
so unlike.

                    *

There is no mantle
and it does not descend.

Self Scrutiny

The threadbare body gathers
with a new consideration
about the hidden bones
that shimmered once like spears
of iris in the mind.

It grows conscious
of its composite parts:
the eyes wet with delicacy
that will yet close
under unopenable marble;

the ear admitting the snarl
of mutabilitie
direct to the brain;
                    the tongue
clung more with understanding

to the roof of the mouth
the more it is loosed
in the savour of freedom
or the curse made flesh;

the thumbs and digits
driven precise into the temples
at the felt limit of our range
as we thunderdrive to Hell

Self Release

Possibly you would rather I stopped
— uttering guttural Christ curses
and destroying my nails down the wall
or dashing myself to pieces once and for all
in a fury beside your head?

I will ease it somehow.
I could pull down a clean knife-shaft
two-handed into the brain and worry it
minutely about until there is
glaze and numbness in 'that' area . . .

Then you would see how charming
it is possible to be,
how recklessly fluent and fascinating,
a startlement to all,
internationally, and beyond.

Self Renewal

Reverently I swung open
the two side mirrors to reveal
everywhere, on a white brow crossed,
two ragged cuts; a wet mouth
held shut; eyes hurt and full.

I peered into these
and their velvet stirred
with the pale secrets of all
the lonely that had ever sat
by their lonely mirrors

studying the lonely shame
that had brought them there to sit
and kiss the icy glass
and recover themselves a little
with icy brow on brow

and one eye cocked at itself
until they felt more able
to slip off about their business
with head held a little higher
and the glass clouding over

the memory of a couple
of fading eye diagrams.

HER VERTICAL SMILE

. . . I remember the elaborate, opulent close of *Der Rosenkavalier* filling the mean little space: the unmade single bed, the dusty electric fire glowing in the grate, spattered with butts, Reidy's narrow unfocused face intent in the dark like an animal. I heard Mahler there for the first time . . .

Overture

For ever and ever
    she wept
for the nth time

overladen with feeling
    and dwelling upon herself
and drawing back

through the luxuriant heavens
    into the light
from whence she came,

the great contralto,
    for her beloved son
pale against the chilly fireplace.

And there goes
    that last lovely heartbeat
of the whole world

like a low terrible string plucked
    Ah Whoom
on the great Harp of Life,

a major triad of strings,
    celestes — trombones! —
released from all earthbound tonalities.

                    *

Will God sit there on the Last Day like that,
    the whole thing played out,
listening to a last echo fade,

staring to one side, just sitting there?
    If only we could wring our talent out,
wring it and wring it dry like that.

A butt flung into a dirty grate.
    Elbows on knees, head bowed
devouring an echo out of nothing.

I

Arms uplifted on the podium,
    the left hand dangling tyrannical;
aetat fünfzig;

the stance flat footed;
    the face a fragile axe,
hard and acid, rapt.

Everything a man can do,
    and more, is done,
the sparse hair thrown back,

the white cuffs flaring,
    the ivory baton flourished
and driven deep.

He sports a little paunch
    but this, in its boxy waistcoat,
merely emphasizes the force of will

we find everywhere
    in his strange work:
the readiness to embrace risk,

tedium, the ignoble,
    to try anything ten times
if so the excessive matter can be settled.

(We have waltzed a while with Disaster,
    coat tails twirling along the precipice,
and She is charmed senseless,

Her harmonies collapse
    at a touch.) Only a double drum
is beating: two hearts coupled.

There is an overpowering tinkle;
    a pregnant hush.
Masterful yet sensitive

his baton explores
    her core of peace,
every rhythm drained

44

into nothing, the nothingness
    adjusting toward
a new readiness.

From his captive hearers
    (though we can scarcely
contain ourselves)

not a cough,
    not a shuffle,
his stance pivotal

above the excited young
    clustered around him
in all our promise,

focused with shining faces
    on the place of measurement itself,
pointing, like children.

Not a stir,
    not a breath,
there at the heart of old Vienna.

*

Overtures and alliances.
    White gloves advance,
decorated bellies retire

down mirrored halls.
    Entente. Volte face.
And seize your partner.

And it's off to the muttonchop slaughter.
    Belted and buttoned brilliant hosts
march to their places line abreast,

bannerets fluttering among their pikes,
    kettledrums beating to match their boots
and, where they halt, to match their pulse,

on a field that will live for ever in glory,
      often as not beside some river,
rivers being natural boundaries

and offering certain useful features
      when the awful day is over.
We might search for harmony there

close up among
      the tangled woebegone
the morning after.

Or we might choose to listen
      down echoing and mirrored walls,
chandelier after trembling chandelier

to the vanishing point,
      with that infinite
imperial Ear

for Whom (a passionate amateur,
      Himself a gifted performer)
our most significant utterances

have been elicited from precisely this matter
      — in ominous drumrolls, slow marches
of tragic penetration,

in blaze of trumpets,
      unstoppable affirmations,
the logic of majesty.

For there are great iron entities
      afloat like towns erect on the water
with new murderous skills,

and there are thunderclouds gathered
      on our perimeter, and the Empire
turns once more toward its farrow.

*

And it is his last year, and the last time
    he is to introduce a new work to us,
and we can tell.

Was there ever one chasm closed
    but another opened
on our case

                — however the medium,
    blood-bearing in itself,
might seem temperate and good?

Or our Music Master
    fold the terms of the curse
back upon itself

in sensible figures in the air
    so the blood might beat at our temples
with the pulse of order

(let it be
    only even as
the work passed)

as though our 'celestial companions'
    shivering all about us in the night
were to slip their mythic roles

and disclose themselves
    with sudden ease as one,
solved in a single figure: The Elect,

a Man and a Woman, the minutiae
    of their breathings together
answered in great glittering systems,

with his hatchet face and rigid rod
    thrown against the blazing heart
in a happy ending.

While as to a beginning
    it is hard to see past
our first parent

patented on his Chapel ceiling
    propped on an elbow,
a languid and burly young man

with everything limply on show,
    and a little out of condition,
finger to finger with God the Father,

the Latter afloat toward him
    with the nub of the matter displaced
in a fold of His purple shift.

Yet enough, surely to that Patriarch-Mother
    — ending or beginning —
that from such thoughts forth

it was only in the excesses of our minds and art
    that we need to undergo
the outrage we appear to find essential.

Allowing always
    for that outrageous rummaging,
breath stopped, pulse paused

in its withheld double dark beat,
    with forces narrowed
in each chosen other.

                            *

For what shall it profit a white gloved
    and glittering bellied elder
puffed sideways at the camera

that mile after drowsy mile
    with bell towers and canals of still water
and deep green laneways doped with living flesh

and town squares cluttered with coffee tables
    and brown brick alleyways teeming
with the ignorant and able young

should darken against themselves,
   and iron animals clamber
in staggered series

up out of the creases and folds
   in our spirits onto dry land
and turn it to mud under us,

and drums burst in ditches at our feet
   and the ghosts of pikes
stutter all around us

and bannerets of our own selves
   dangle on wires along
irregular rivers of our own making,

so that upon a fixed hour
   a long horn will honk
and the field is his or another's

and ground breezes pick their ways
   across its brimming puddles
and into its unnatural lairs?

There are photographs
   of the sudden peace:
the late enemies together like family groups

half leaning against one another.
   There is a heavy boot in one
actually standing on a fallen hand.

Intermezzo

Munich
— December 1914

To —

My dear Sir, and Warrior,
  I was filled with inadequacy and shame
when they told me you had marched away.

I have set my mind now
  — since I can offer nothing else —
to the service of the German cause.

For I believe it is important
  to articulate and ennoble these happenings
and give them meaning.

How will it all end?
  The anxiety, the curiosity,
are immense. But is there not

a joy in the curiosity?
  That all things will be made new
by this profound and powerful event

and the German people emerge from it
  stronger and prouder,
freer and happier?

Grant it may be so.
  All hail and victory,
my dear Herr Doktor.

I pray your Christmas
  will have a strange beauty
in these harsh circumstances.

I take your hand in friendship
  and remain
gratefully yours,

T — M —

II

A step forward and a lesser
  step back, the baton withdrawn.
A timed excision.

'Glockenspiel!'
  The bony left fingers
prise it open.

'Tuba! Double basses!'
  There is a prolonged emptying
of the writhing contents.

'Trumpets and drenching strings!'
  Is there anything quite like
getting to the root?

Dolce . . . He reaches
  for something soothing.
His shoulders sag for a bar of silence.

But why is there no ease?
  For something magnuscule has been accomplished;
the entities that made it possible

are locked together still;
  they have not even
begun to look at one another.

He stirs on his pinnacle.
  He is summoning
the ghost of a double beat,

a felt weight on the ear,
  fishchill,
a remote stink

from the depths,
  news ascending
speechless from a lower cold

where the senses have no function.
    It assumes a body.
It is a brute bobbin

throwing a hard shade
    backward and down,
and spearing upward

with dead eye and hacked downlaugh
    and slope of hide
shimmering with instincts

toward a glitter of tiny voices
    whispering among themselves:
I am! I am!

*

And indeed you are
    — teeming everywhere
with your aches and needs

along our bloody passageways,
    knocking against one another
in never ending fuss

as if there were no matching
    and more than matching
voracious peace.

Mind minnows
    with flickering
intelligence-flecks for faces;

carrion swarming to fill
    every pulse passing
in unsureness or error;

now, before we suffer Her
    to gather us once more
into Her farewell and for ever,

I wag this pale finger
    down among you
in promise

(fuss
    propped upon promise
implying purpose,

waste
    a part of the process,
implying life):

that there is an outer carrion
    bone-walking in a dream bedlam,
half lit, idling

in foul units,
    circling our furthest reach
with a refusing snarl,

and that from even this matter
    (as of man's head rammed against stone
and woman a mad animal)

we might yet make a gavotte
    to feed
that everlasting Ear.

*

It is absolutely Heavenly:
    the very first morning.
All the strings are agreed.

Our couple are taking the air
    by the sea side,
content in their own sweet silence,

at arm's length
    — it is ocean and earth
that are touching.

In the faded photo the sea surface
   is sheer silver,
not one rock

to break the abstract
   mathematics of the brine,
or that a temptress

might clamber up
   and slither onto
to try out a throaty call.

She accompanies him
   on the ribbed and running salt sand,
skirted full length,

stamped blank
   under her black broad-brimmed hat,
coupling her attentive shadow with his

as he strolls in his tight trousers,
   jabbing sandworms and brooding
how to respond,

how to admire the solid beloved.
   Morning . . .
A shimmering calm . . .

A little wind
   disturbing what there is of hair . . .
Very well.

Let the Fall begin,
   the whole wide
landscape descend gently

— the open air
   a single throat
thrown wide

in a gasp of
   alarm and praise —
and a portal close.

And there ought to be
  a good deal of wandering
and seeking for peace

and desire of one kind and another,
  with the throat employed
for its own lovely sake

in moving utterances
  made of the simplest poetry.
Good man-made matter

is best for our design:
  forest murmurs; a tired horseman
drinking in friendship and farewell;

voices blurred in longing;
  renewal in Beauty;
Earth's pale flowers blossoming

in a distance turning to pure light
  shining blue
for ever and for ever.

And central to the Song's force
  an awareness
(in the actual motions of the mouth,

the intimacy of
  its necessary movements)
of her two nutrient smiles:

the one with lips pouted soft
  in half wet love
in earnest of

that other,
  dwelling upon itself for ever,
her vertical smile.

Coda

Nine are the enabling elements
    in the higher crafts
and the greatest of these is Luck.

I lift my
    baton and my
trousers fall.

OUT OF IRELAND

... the perfection of their art seems to lie in their concealing it, as if 'it were the better for being hidden. An art revealed brings shame.' Hence it happens that the very things that afford unspeakable delight to the minds of those who have a fine perception and can penetrate carefully to the secrets of the art, bore, rather than delight, those who have no such perception — who look without seeing, and hear without being able to understand. When the audience is unsympathetic they succeed only in causing boredom with what appears to be but confused and disordered noise ...

GIRALDUS CAMBRENSIS on Irish music

Entrance

Crows scoured the wet evening clean
above our heads.

Two languages interchanged.

We came to a halt
with our half-certainties:

*that love is
to clasp simply,
question fiercely;*

and the artistic act . . .
long library bodies, their pens
distinct against the sinking sun.

Native Wisdom

We leaned against the rain-spitted wind
and got the gate open
into the churchyard.

A flat root of stone
lay like a tongue
in the coarse grass.

Medals and beads and bits of mirror
by the hooded well, a clip shimmering
in the water, the pious litter gave witness.

A crow scuffled in the hedge
and floated out with a dark groan
toward the church tower,

and flapped onto
the parapet:
I am native born in this place.

I have knowledge
of flesh and blood.
Come and buy.

Half way up the church wall
the Black Robber
stretched out his neck and stared:

Give ear to him and he will fill it
with nothing but white rubbish.
I am native born

in your foul deeds.
Good and evil
come and buy.

On an oval stone
set over the window
she crossed her thin arms downward

and offered her opened self:
This swallows them both
and all the questions.

Here you are native born.
Yes and no
Come here and buy.

Rough stones stood everywhere
tilted in a soil
thick with re-burials,

with a hole half open
in the ground like a mouth
at the foot of one of them:

I am born again in the spirit.
So shall you be. Love is all
or nothing. Come and buy.

Harmonies

Seamus of the Smart Suit, box player, made
signals to us across the grass tussocks and graves
the day we all came down from Cork
to commemorate our musical friend.

By Gobnait's sculpted lump
— a slab of a woman on a frieze
of stone buds and the locked bodies of bees —
he struggled in his nose with English,

showing the Holy Stations and instructing
with rigid finger and embarrassed snorts,
his box squeezed shut back in the house
with Mairtín's pipes and the pair of fiddles,

the same instruments, ranging together
in natural sweetness, with a many-sounded
and single voice, that gave Iohannes Scotus
— Eriugena, and instructing the known world —

his harmonious certainty: that the world's parts,
ill-fitted in their stresses and their pains,
will combine at last in polyphonic sweet-breathing union
and all created Nature ascend like joined angels,

limbs and bodies departing the touch of Earth
static in a dance of return, all Mankind gathered
stunned at the world's edge
silent in a choir of understanding.

The Furnace

Imperishable creatures
returning into God's light.
A resurrection, not a vanishing.

Intensifying, as iron
melts in the furnace
— intensified into flowing fire,

aching for a containing Shape.
Eriugena's notion matching
my half-baked, bodily own,

who have *consigned*
my designing will stonily
to your flames

and will turn again toward the same furnace
that melted the union of our will
to ineffable zero

how many times in its radiant clasp
(a cancellation
certainly speechless for a minute or two)

in token of the Union and the Light.
Until gender returned
and we were made two again

Male and Female
in punishment for Man's will
and reminded of our Fall.

In token of which
I plant this dry kiss
in your rain-wet hair.

The Dance

It is the staling music of memory
has brought us nosing once more
around our forgotten young hero

and his high-spirited doings.
Grieving solos fade
and twine on echoes of each other

down the shallow valley:
his own voices,
divided against themselves.

His spirit, in one piece still
(just for a little while,
and only just)

is cavorting in answer
all brains and bare feet
along the scruffy skyline,

stepping the parish boundary
in goodbye
and beckoning with a comical thumb

up over the edge:
*Come and buy
my terrible new capabilities* . . .

The little plants shivering
green and pale on the far slope
in a breeze out of the Next Testament,

unplaceable, familiar smells
stealing among the goats'
dainty, unbothered feet.

And there would be no sign
if we tried to follow
his shifting rhythms,

the throaty piping,
the dry taps fractured on the drum skin,
the delicate new hooves

on approval, slithering to the beat
down out of sight
into the stony places.

The Land of Loss

Nothing certain of this world,
Iohannes teaches,
except for certain impediments
we might carry with ourselves:

our legs bound, for our failure
to walk in the Divine Law;
our hands hindered, for their hesitation
in virtuous deeds;

and it grows dark and we stumble
in gathering ignorance
in a land of loss
and unfulfillable desire.

He himself was driven out of France
and half way home
for heresy.

He taught in the Abbey at Malmesbury
and died there
at his students' hands.

They stabbed him
with their pens
because he made them think.

Exit

Lidless, lipless, opensocketed
and dumb with suspended understanding,
waiting for the Day,

our best evidence
is aligned all about under us,
their figures finished.

The dance is at our own feet.
Give me your hand.
A careful step

together over that outstuck
tongue, and shut this gate
in God's name

behind us, once and for all.
And reach me my weapon
in the goat-grey light.

ST CATHERINE'S CLOCK

'. . . chosen and lifted up against the light
for the Fisherman's thumb
and the bowel-piercing hook.'

The whole terrace
slammed shut.
I inhaled the granite lamplight,
divining the energies of the prowler.

A window opposite, close up.
In a corner, a half stooped image
focused on the intimacy
of the flesh of the left arm.

The fingers of the right hand are set
in a scribal act on the skin:
a gloss, simple and swift as thought,
is planted there.

The point uplifted,
wet with understanding,
he leans his head a moment
against the glass.

I see.

Thomas Street at the first hour.

The clock
on the squat front of St Catherine's
settled a gilded point
up soundless into place.

1803

After the engraving by George Cruikshank

Lord Kilwarden, genuflected
prim and upset outside his carriage door,
thrown back rhetorical

among a pack of hatted simians,
their snouted malice gathered
into the pike-point entering his front.

His two coachmen
picked, like his horses, from a finer breed
register extremes of shocked distress.

Somewhere a nephew,
Mr Richard Wolfe, is fallen
and spilling his share of blood and matter.

From a non-contemporary nationalist artist's impression

And Robert Emmet on the scaffold high,
as close as possible to the site of the outrage,
is dropped from his brief height

into a grove of redcoats
mounted with their rumps
toward a horrified populace.

The torch of friendship and the lamp of life
extinguished, his race finished,
the idol of his soul offered up,

sacrificed on the altar of truth and liberty,
awaiting the cold honours of the grave,
requiring only the charity of silence,

he has done.
The sentence pronounced in the usual form,
he has bowed and retired.

The pasty head is separated and brandished aloft,
the dead forehead with the black wet lock
turned toward the Fountain.

1792
Jas. Malton, del.

At the drink shop by the Church corner
two horsemen are greeting,
their mounts brow to brow.

In the background
some activity about the water fountain:
a pair of children or dwarfs,

a man and women with buckets,
a couple of mongrels
worrying the genitals out of each other.

Centre, barefoot,
bowed in aged rags to the earth,
a hag

toils across the street
on her battered business,
a drained backside

turned toward St Catherine;
everybody, even those
most near, turned away.

Right foreground, a shade waits for her
against a dark cart humped man-shaped
with whipstaff upright.

Set down to one side
by unconcerned fingers, a solitary redcoat
is handling the entire matter.

Past the Watch House and Watling Street
beyond St James's Gate, a pale blue
divides downhill into thin air

on a distant dream
of Bow Lane
and Basin Lane.

73

1938

Two red-and-black matched silky-decorated
tin boxes out of India
fit beside each other behind her
up on the tea shelf, behind her head.

The shoulders of the black iron-flowered
weighing-scales on the counter
balance, embossed, across the socket-top of the stand.
The brass plates hang, equal, in their chains.

Round ounce weights
and multiples and little
black fractions nestle
on one another against the base.

Her knuckles and waxy nails took hold
of the counter-lid
and pulled it back up
against the square glass jars

of silver and black eyeballs
and glassy twisted coloured sticks.
She had a fat sugar sack,
with the twiny neck rolled back,

tucked in against her high stool
and the black boot laced up
under her skirt and the black beads
hanging down over her brown apron.

In on a dark shelf
on the way into the back
she had the goose eggs from down the country,
green and big, the fill of your palm.

*

Aunty Gertie shuffled
across the scullery. She had
big slippers and a slow bum.

Little Uncle Ned was always in and out
grinning at her. (Uncle Larry said
she could stick him in her pocket.)

She could let a long belch
up her neck, like a noise
coming up out of a jug.

*

I was inside in the back room
up on the bed with a rolled-up newspaper
at the holy picture, killing flies.

The whole bed
gave when I moved across it
in the pillow smell.

There was one on the glass
on the Sacred Heart's face,
with the black little pointed head

and dead eyes
looking everywhere.
It kept twining and wiping its thin paws.

But somebody in the other room
shouted: 'Go on out
and tell your Aunty Cis we want her'

and it disappeared, and started flying
up with the others around and around
at angles under the bulb.

*

75

Sometimes some of the aunts
wouldn't talk for weeks,
in a bad temper after passing remarks.

They chewed their teeth
and passed each other by
with their glasses and stiff faces.

But some of them would keep muttering
together in the middle room.
And then someone one day suddenly

would laugh up out of her throat,
and all the put-on pain and the high snout
would go out of their stares.

*

Up the bright road starting toward Naas
with the line of new houses
going up the long hill
into the country

near the big white Chapel
with the two spires
towering up off the front wall
full of arches and holy figures and stone flowers

we turned off into a hidden
street of brown houses
down to a door in the quietest corner
to visit our best cousins,

older, handsome boys, all with fine teeth,
all three of them doing well,
two of them always
very understanding and good.

*

We shouted everywhere at one another
— even in whispers, out over the river brink,

holding onto the rushes, hardly breathing
down through our shadows into the water

for the sign of a striped perch pretending
among the reeds or sheltering against the bank,

to see it move, and drop a stone in
scattering our faces.

*

The Night crept
among our chalk signs on the path
and trickled into the shores.

The moon hung round and silver
out over the empty Back
between the backs of the people's houses

where we piled the rubbish up
on the clay in the dark
and set it on fire and talked into the flames

and skipped around in wickedness
with no mercy to the weak or the fat
or the witless or the half blind.

*

I have struggled, hand
over hand,
in the savage dance.

I have lain inert, the flesh in nightmare,
eating and eaten,
with eyes wide open.

The balm of a clouded breast . . .
The musk of a stocking rolled down
over her pale knee beside the fire-place.

Then left by myself
sitting up in the fire shadows,
little fingertip touches

flickering reddened
over my picture book.
I let them,

and let it fall after a while
and the security of love
found a place in my marrow.

A little boy, some kind of an uncertain
shade, started trying to get up
with wings dragging.

Then upright in beauty,
his pinions touched with the red firelight.
He turned his golden head.

But when I woke again it was all restless
with the stare of love's hatred
and you that know well and will not know

and ill-will spitting
casual at the street corner, ignorant
born and bred.

And I have sat solitary
outside, on the low window-sill,
a brutal nail nagging out of nowhere.

*

Sometimes it sounded like she was giving out
but she was really minding us.

I know I was not bold
even if I did terrible things.

I was not a barefaced liar
or a thick-ah or a go-boy, or a pup.

I never went with the cur next door
or those gets down the street.

I was always properly dressed,
and minded my brother.

One night we scrounged up together
and felt the little eggs in each other.

And I always remembered
who and what I am.

Grand Canal Place,
  at the second hour.
Live lights on oiled water
  in the terminus harbour.

Not fifty yards from here
she took the certificate
and slapped it down on the table.
It took that to shut them up.

Kathleen was very good
and Matty kindness itself.
With three sons of their own
they put her up for the birth.

Nurse Fitzsimons looked after her
out of the long bag. She was very fat
and looked after the whole neighbourhood
for twenty years afterwards.

*

His voice, empty and old,
came around to it more than once:
something about the family
he had to tell me sometime.

A dead voice now
in my ear: You can be certain
from your own cold certainties
that you are a son of hers.

But you would have to try
very far under my feeble force
to find anything more
than a passing kind of doggedness.

Closer than a brother
(born of the same woman,
face down face up to her fondness,
and a quiet brutal other

closer than a brother)
look for the dimpled smile
empty of understanding
that will tell you the rest of it.

I leave you a few faint questions
and good and bad example
and things I have not told you,
and who and what you are.

*

Bridie, the next and youngest,
the musical one of the family,
was hardly like an aunt at all,

bright and sharp, so unlucky
with her first love lost or dead
in Rio de Janeiro.

She knelt down quickly beside me
with her handbag and her schoolteacher's smile
for a hurried hug and goodbye,

the pair of us so alike,
everybody agreed,
wherever we got our brains.

Thomas Street.
As far as we can reach.
Turning a night face

and thin hair feeling the wet
from the Fountain
and some that are most near.

A modest bloody little trickle
is spilling this way and that
from the foot of the ghost of the scaffold

inching to the left,
starting down with the hill slope,
sensing the possibility of direction

— ghost handkerchiefs
dipped with tears, in communion,
in its course —

and sensing the far-off
impossible magnificat: a river
coiling its potent flood

between high salt block walls,
carrying a brand new soul
struggling with wet wings

to flourish a while in freedom
on the surface of our recollection
— not anchored in our angry hearts —

till it come to some more friendly port
to give it shelter against the heavy storms
with which it is buffeted.

Long-lost, a second-last letter,
written almost in his own tears,
was found years afterward
in the stuffing of a sofa.

*

On the right,
up in the slatted turret,
a tooth on the big measuring wheel

re-engaged,
protestant,
inch by inch.

1740

About the third hour.

Ahead, at the other end
of the darkened market place
a figure crossed over

out of Francis Street
reading the ground, all dressed up
in black, like a madwoman.

Out of Ireland: Precedents and Notes

St Gobnait's Graveyard, Ballyvourney

. . . The gate creaked in the dusk. The trampled grass,
soaked and still, was disentangling
among the standing stones
after the day's excess.

A flock of crows circled
the church tower, scattered
and dissolved chattering
into the trees. Fed . . .

> From *A Selected Life:*
> *In Memory of Seán Ó Riada,* 1972

. . . Laws of order I find I have discovered
mainly at your hands . . . of failure and increase,
the stagger and recovery of spirit:

. . . That love is to clasp simply, question fiercely . . .

*

Fragility echoing fragilities
From whom I have had every distinctness . . .

. . . I consign my designing will stonily
To your flames . . .

> From *Phoenix Park,* 1968

. . . I believe now that love is half persistence,
A medium in which, from change to change,
Understanding may be gathered . . .

> From *Nightwalker,* 1967

Ballyvourney

A town and place of pilgrimage in the Sullane river valley in the Irish-speaking
area of West Cork. The grave of the seventh-century St Gobnait is in the church
grounds, with her holy well and other Christian remains, still visited as part of
the 'pattern' on her feast day, 11 February. The medieval church building has a
grotesque head in the tower wall and a *sheela-na-gig* — an obscene cult or
fertility figure — displayed in a depression above a window in the South wall.
There is a modern statue by the sculptor Seamus Murphy which incorporates a

swarm of bees, associated with the Saint in folklore. The composer and musician Seán Ó Riada, who settled in Coolea in 1964, is buried in the churchyard.

Scoti

... Carolingian educational policies had a well-defined and limited goal: to create a clergy capable of guiding the people. However, the ultimate results surpassed the initial aim, to constitute what has been called the Carolingian Renaissance ... in the middle of the eighth to the end of the ninth century, literary production was greater than it had ever been before in the northern domains ...

... the literary revival was animated by a group of Irish (*Scoti*): Clement and Dungal at Charlemagne's court; Dicuil, who followed the lead of another Irishman, Virgil of Salzburg, in his interest in cosmography; Sedulius Scotus, who arrived in Liège about 874; and, above all, John Scotus Eriugena whose very name proclaims his Irish birthplace. A protégé of Charles the Bald, John, with other Scots, revived the school of Laon, making it a center of Greek studies and philosophy. The Irish were astonishing, sometimes even scandalous, because of their free speech, worldly science, and intellectual audacity. These were incomparably learned men. They cried out to a crowd of customers, 'If anyone desires wisdom, let him come to us and receive it, for we are here to sell it.' ... Relations were sometimes strained ... They were jealous of one another, digging at one another in epigrams and accusing one another of doctrinal deviations ...

From *Daily Life in the World of Charlemagne*.
Pierre Riché, trans. Jo Ann McNamara. University
of Pennsylvania Press, 1978

Polyphony

... The music of antiquity and of the ancient Church knew neither harmony nor polyphony; it was essentially of the kind that is known to us from plain chant.

... Polyphony originated in the north and north-west of Europe. Its most primitive form was probably the *baritus* or *barditus* of the ancient Germans, that terrifying battle-cry of which Tacitus and other ancient writers make mention. In the literature on musical theory, the earliest treatise on polyphony is, in all probability, the so-called *Musica Enchiriadis* ... John Scotus, in the third book of his *Periphyseon*, illustrates the meaning and function of contraries in created nature by a comparison taken from music, which describes a similar form of polyphony as that of the *Musica Enchiriadis* (iii 6):

> For as instrumental music is composed of notes of different length and quality (pitch), which, heard in isolation, differ considerably according to tension, but if they are combined variously in certain relations according to

the rules of musical theory result in sounds of a natural sweetness, so also the unity of the universe is made up of the parts, dissonant from one another when considered separately, yet of one all-embracing nature.

The impression that John Scotus is thinking of a type of music which he knew from his native country is confirmed by a comparison of this passage with the description of Irish musicians and their art by Giraldus Cambrensis (iii. 13):

It is only in the case of musical instruments that I find any commendable diligence in this people. They seem to me to be incomparably more skilled in these than any other people that I have seen. The movement is . . . quick and lively, while at the same time the melody is sweet and pleasant. It is remarkable how in spite of the great speed of the fingers, the musical proportion is maintained. The melody is kept perfect and full with unimpaired art through everything — through quivering measures and the involved use of several instruments — with a rapidity that charms, a rhythmic pattern that is varied, and a concord achieved through elements discordant. They harmonize at intervals of the octave and the fifth, but they always begin with B flat and with a B flat end, so that everything may be rounded with the sweetness of charming sonority. They glide so subtly from one mode to another, and the grace notes so freely sport with such abandon and bewitching charm around the steady tone of the heavier sound, that the perfection of their art seems to lie in their concealing it . . .

From *Ireland: Harbinger of the Middle Ages*
Ludwig Bieler. Oxford University Press, 1963

April 19, 1958. Today we heard a record of Gregorian chants. Although primarily an expression of the piety of the early Middle Ages, they are at the same time, in their slightly monotonous quality, evidence of the unspoiled capacity for emotion that people had in those times. Stronger stimuli were not needed. In the painting of the age, also, small gestures sufficed to express drama. And recently I read that people fainted when they first heard early polyphony. Thus progress can also be understood as impoverishment.

From *Spandau: The Secret Diaries*. Albert Speer,
trans. Richard and Clara Winston. Collins, 1976

The Return

. . . Finally, all nature itself and its causes will be moved towards God. God will be all in all . . .

In this return the substance of things does not perish, but moves upwards to the better . . . The intelligible body does not cease in the higher, as molten iron does not cease in fire, or air in light; but it is further on the way of return . . .

*

... The deified will ascend through innumerable steps of divine contemplation so as to see God in the glass of divine fantasy. The reprobate will descend through the diverse descents of their vices into the depths of ignorance and exterior darkness ... The binding of the legs of the reprobate typifies their difficulty in walking in the divine law; the binding of their hands, their difficulty in doing virtuous acts ...

*

... Eriugena sides with Gregory of Nyssa in surmising that the division into sexes was in punishment of man's perverse will ...

From Eriugena. John J. O'Meara. Cultural Relations
Committee/The Mercier Press, 1969

'Give me your hand'

'Tabhair dom do lámh': This is the title of an early seventeenth-century Irish air — often given in the Latin, 'Da mihi manum' — composed by the harper Ruairi Dall, 'the Blind', of the princely Northern family of the Uí Catháin.

89

OXFORD POETS

Fleur Adcock

James Berry

Edward Kamau Brathwaite

Joseph Brodsky

Michael Donaghy

D. J. Enright

Roy Fisher

David Gascoyne

David Harsent

Anthony Hecht

Zbigniew Herbert

Thomas Kinsella

Brad Leithauser

Herbert Lomas

Derek Mahon

Medbh McGuckian

James Merrill

John Montague

Peter Porter

Craig Raine

Tom Rawling

Christopher Reid

Stephen Romer

Carole Satyamurti

Peter Scupham

Penelope Shuttle

Louis Simpson

Anne Stevenson

George Szirtes

Anthony Thwaite

Charles Tomlinson

Chris Wallace-Crabbe

Hugo Williams

also

Basil Bunting

W. H. Davies

Keith Douglas

Ivor Gurney

Edward Thomas